scar tissue

Maiden Voices is a new series introducing a brand-new concept: books written by young women for young adults, male and female, exploring their lives, hopes, aspirations, anxieties, joys, dreams...

Nikhat Grewal is a child psychologist and aspiring fiction writer and traveller. She believes in the power of bed tea, human weakness and lunar eclipses. She lives in New Delhi with her turtles, in a flat she sometimes shares with her dog.

MAIDEN VOICES

scar tissue

8 lives, 8 young women

edited by

nikhat grewal

women UNLIMITED
an associate of
kali for women

Scar Tissue: 8 Lives, 8 Young Women
was first published in 2007 by

Women Unlimited
(an associate of Kali for Women)
K-36, Hauz Khas Enclave, Ground Floor
New Delhi 110 016

ISBN: 8188965-33-2

Cover design: Alpana Khare

Typeset at Print Services, B-17 Lajpat Nagar-II,
New Delhi 110 024
and printed at Pauls Press, E-44/11, Okhla Phase-II,
New Delhi 110 020

Contents

acknowledgements

To my mother, who pokes and prods and makes me believe. Ritu Menon, who first told me I could string a sentence together. Niharika for being so patient as I growled through the edits. And to all the other women in my life—Raws, Ames, Mayapots, Nin, Sak, Sib, Trish, Rags, Dev, V, Kate, Angel, Samiha, Bunny, Runi masi, Jo masi, Pincha masi, Laila Khala, Nani, Alps—thank you for being the smartest, funniest and most stylish ones.

For Shokeen Dev Solanki, my best friend.

introduction

The enormity of this book and of the responsibility of putting it together did not hit me until I started to write this introduction. What I did by collecting these eight essays is not extraordinary. What is, are the stories that I was let into in the process. Who are the girls whose stories you will be reading? We are the ones you see driving to work, whistling down an auto, sipping cosmopolitans at a bar, catching the film festival at Siri Fort Auditorium or drinking coffee and laughing loudly in a café. What do we have in common? Our economic stratum (upper middle class), our hopes, dreams, fears and a certain glint in the eye.

Thirty-five years ago things were different for girls like us in India. A marriage and a career as a teacher or nurse was as good as it got, though if you were really 'fast', you could be an air hostess.

It took a long hard battle fought by our mothers in the '70's and '80's for us to now stand on our own as a group. Today I can be a lesbian peace corps. worker leaving for Iraq and I dare anyone to do anything about it. Yes, we are here. No, we are not the new Indian women. We are the old model but with voices that can ring loud and clear, carrying far into the distance.

The battle is far from over though. It was a year ago that I started to look for women between the ages of eighteen and thirty to write for this book. I met with many, some of whom wrote down their stories and yet would not publish them. Not because they were afraid but because they chose to keep some things personal and to tell their stories only to a few. It does not matter because the process helped them all and the idea of the book seemed to give them courage. Some realised they were better writers than they thought and others just saw things more clearly. And then there were those with an amazing story to tell, but who felt that they could not share it. What really amazed ... angered ... me was that it was not that these women lacked the strength to speak of their own lives freely. They have the courage and the voice but they cannot go public. Why not? To protect their parents, their families and their boyfriends, of course. What is it about a liberated woman who speaks her mind that still embarrasses and scares others so much? So is it the same old story being enacted in modern settings? No, each time my heart broke for one girl's silence, the voice of another would restore my faith that things have changed. Young women in India today are strong, unafraid and doing it for themselves.

The women whose stories you will read ...

Amrita. Who acknowledges the limitations of first her biological father and then her stepfather and finds strength and solace in her relationship with her sister.

Phoenix, the girl who chose that name because writing her story changed the way in which she looked at herself. The first piece that she wrote spoke only of one disastrous man after another. It was only after she read her own piece out loud that she realised that this was not her, that these men did not define her life. So, out came the black marker and the piece was re-written. I saw the phoenix reemerge from the ashes. Thank you for your realisation, it was mine as well.

Or Deveshe whom I never met and yet who trusted me enough to share her story with me via email. Her quest for experience and answers mirrors a lot of our own. The true enjoyment of her freedom diffused through her confusion offers us comfort that yes, we may not know what we really want but getting there can be fun.

Alankrita who vocalised her thoughts by asking questions, and sometimes answering them with intelligence and passion herself. Is wanting and fighting for one's own rightful place being a feminist? Or is it just human nature? As Alankrita points out, what does shaving one's legs or not have to do with it all?

We don't want to look like men, we don't want to act like men, we just want to be unafraid.

Tilly—thank you for pointing out that we all don't have to be thespians to act and to play different parts in our 'real lives'. It is easy to get lost in the midst of expectations and limitations, both our own and of those we love. We are all a little schizophrenic, trying to pick what fits us best. Especially now, as this new breed of young women emerges, if one looks deeply, the worker, the lover, the mother, the sister, the courtesan, the vulnerable, the strong—she is in us all.

I then marvel at the power and courage of Anonymous as she cries out aloud at the hypocrisy of her freedom. It is through her words that I felt the sanctity of my own body for the first time. Here is a girl, smart, loving, fearless and yet she is unable to claim even an acknowledgement of the violations she repeatedly suffers. Signing her own name to her story seems like a distant prospect.

And then Mukulika, who I sometimes feel has written the most complex piece of all. Feeling what most of us have felt at one point or may feel again—discontent, feeling wrong when everything seems right. Angry yet smiling, tired but dancing, aching to soar above what is. Fly, Mukulika, put down that Magharita and fly.

Writing my own piece, I realised exactly what a difficult task I had asked of these women. To write down one's experiences concisely and coherently in 3000 to 4000 words is a hard thing to do indeed. There were times when I wanted to stop, scared and unwilling to share myself. Truthfully, it was the courage and honesty of the other women that inspired me to continue. Writing my story I felt sad for the girl I lost and yet writing those last hopeful lines, I surprised myself. The hope is instinctual and the anticipation of laughter natural. Through my story I did realise, I believe that I will be happy.

So, are we really liberated? Are we any different from the girls our mothers were? The biggest gift the women here have given me is a definite answer to that question. Yes we are. I look around when I walk down the street, when I am in a market place or at a book reading. I see the excited, intelligent, beautiful faces of the women around me and my heart swells with pride. I am proud to be a part of you. We may still have a long way to go. Battles to fight for ourselves but we have choices and we choose to exercise them. So these are our stories and perhaps some of yours, as well.

the story of me

amrita

Confusion. Chaos. And then the words start coming out, crystal clear. Only in my mind, of course. At first, I used to think it was just me—you know the feeling—rebel without much of a cause in this heartless world, where everyone else is so normal it's almost sickening. Where you figure you should be put away in a straitjacket for your thoughts. A great deal of experience later, you realize you're not alone. You're not the only twisted soul. Everyone's got a story. Here is mine.

Ever since I was pretty young, I've been one of those world-weary, cynical types. I'm sure there's a perfectly sound explanation for this, but I prefer to think I'm an ancient, an old soul. Just doing my time before finally attaining nirvana. Not that I believe in rebirth. Or even death, for that matter. I think you go on doing your thing, it's just that one day people stop noticing you—the Hollow Man effect.

I've been very Hollow Man-ish myself. It's not that people don't notice me; it's just that very few really know me, if you get what I mean. But what the hell?! It's been rough at times, but I lived through my childhood and I lived through adolescence, so I'm pretty sure I'll be able to tackle whatever comes my way.

I used to ignore a lot of things. I just refused to think about who I was and where I was coming from. But that's not right. All the negativity bottled inside needs a vent. This piece is symbolic—it's sort of my coming to terms with the child I once was. I'd just like to start out by making it clear that although this is personal, it is not a sob story. I'm not angling for sympathy. This came about after a great deal of introspection, and it has helped me deal with my inner demons and move on with my life.

To start at the beginning, my mother married the wrong guy. It was an arranged marriage, as was common in that generation. She got divorced from this horribly abusive, alcoholic bastard (that would be my biological father) after some seven years of misery. I was around four at the time. My sister, being two years older than me, was at once tormentor and best friend. We're still best friends, and I probably torment her more than anything ... Anyway, the two of us lived with my grandparents for about a year, while my mom tried to earn a living. I missed my mom. A lot. I don't even know if I missed my dad. I remember him making mom cry by beating the crap out of her, so ... I guess not.

My sister was (and still is) my guardian angel. Somehow she would always explain things to me, and make me feel all right. She is one amazing person. I mean without her, I probably wouldn't be alive today. I definitely would not have made it this far in life. (exactly how far that is is a totally different story).

I remember meeting one of my mother's friends, Shiv Uncle, for the first time. He was really sweet, and a lot of fun. He was actually her boyfriend from back when they were both in college. Soon enough, he became my dad. More real than the biological one. If this were a Hollywood script, I'd end here, telling you that life was just 'peachy' after that.

But it wasn't. It sure was a lot better than what came before that, but that's not saying much at all. The cool part was my dad's job. He's a diplomat, so we immediately set off on this global adventure that has been my life (at least, until I landed in Welham in the eleventh grade). The uncool part is that my family was in denial. While my sister and I were growing up, divorce was like the F-word. I started swearing in second grade, but that's beside the point.

I think that had a lot to do with how we all turned out—the denial bit, I mean, not the swearing. We never faced our problems. My sister and I were always conspiring (and fighting!), but there wasn't that much we could understand at that age. The family was a bit twisted and had its share of issues, which we never discussed.

There is a lot of strange stuff buried in the past, somewhere. I used to steal. From stores. I got caught once, but I got away after my sister covered for me. I don't know how convincing the story was, but again, my parents never thought to confront the deeper issue. Of why I wanted to steal. Of how it was hard to fit in at school at first. We had funny accents, funny clothes, and less of an allowance than other kids ... let's not forget that there are a LOT of spoiled children in these international schools.

I used to cry a great deal when I was a kid. I'm not sure exactly when I stopped (led to, perhaps, by various insulting jokes at my expense), but that's when I began to internalize everything. I would store up all this hurt. It's only pretty recently, at the grand old age of twenty, that I've rediscovered the art of crying. The funny part is that now I can cry pretty much on demand, much to the boyfriend's horror!

I think I started operating on two levels around the time I stopped crying. There was the private me, then rose this protective wall, and then the public me. So although everyone knew me as this pudgy, bubbly, popular kid, this was definitely a distorted view. Well, except the pudgy part.

I used to enjoy going to school. It had this fairy-tale sheen on it (okay, maybe not the homework and the surprise tests). I liked being around people. I loved the way they were so normal. In hindsight, I realize that they probably weren't, but that is what I used to think, anyway.

Thanks to us moving every couple of years, I learned to adapt to new situations pretty fast. I was a sort of chameleon. I could fit myself in different, multi-cultural groups. I never stuck around in one group for too long, though, so I guess I'm part gypsy as well as part ancient.

Another reason I liked school was that I used to feel smart. I'd get good grades and all that. My teachers and even some of my friends would be impressed. At home, of course, it was another story. I was never smart enough, I was way too lazy, and I was seen as one of the mindless MTV brigade. I don't think my parents could even stand me when I was growing up. In their eyes, I had all the makings of a bum.

I can see why, though. My sister is a near-genius. She managed both worlds pretty comfortably. She studied and partied (as much as she could get away with, anyway), and even kept the peace in the family. Particularly important when it came to me getting dumped on. It wasn't easy, and she put up with a lot. Like I told you, she's an angel.

My parents—I don't think I'll ever be able to figure out why they used to be so strange, I say 'used to be', because they have definitely mellowed. This is a welcome change, though probably too late for my sister and me. I so hope it's been in time for my little brother. I haven't mentioned him yet, but he is such a ray of sunshine. He's eleven years younger than me (you do the math and figure it out!), and definitely has a more mature mind. Okay, maybe I've pushed it. He has seen a lot though, and sometimes he says things that really choke me up. I tell you I just cannot pray hard enough for him.

My parents were very strict with us, but they have eased up a bit on my brother. I'm not comparing them to typical orthodox Indian parents, because then they would probably sound like God's gift to teenagers. But they were much stricter than you would imagine. They didn't like sleepovers, phone conversations, they didn't like the idea of boyfriends, or even guy friends, no parties, no drinking, all that. Quite a bummer, really. I understand now that they were trying to instill a sense of responsibility in us, but it certainly did not make life any easier.

I don't know, but that is probably why my sister and I are so close today. It could have easily gone the other way though, with us hating each other, but thank God for small mercies!

What really got me down about our family life was the bitching. The fighting. The screaming. The hitting. Sure, I understand that my parents had issues. And mood swings. But why exactly did we have to be dragged into every little fight? Believe me, the battle lines were clearly drawn early on. I was always to be on my mom's side, and my sister was on my dad's. As a result, none of us had a functional relationship with each other for the better part of a decade. So much for emotional manipulation.

At times I thought of suicide, but then I figured that life could only get better. When my sister left for college though, that was the last straw. I couldn't see myself surviving in the war zone without her. I prayed my ass off: I pleaded, whined, and even threatened God that I would kill myself if there was no divine intervention. Somehow my father's transfer was stopped mid-way, and I was packed off to boarding school.

Once I got to Welham, I began to think that God was pulling a fast one on me. It took me some time to adjust to things. There was the culture shock, there was the cold porridge, and 'leather' toast. All of a sudden, my family life seemed appealing, and I (shock, horror) even started to miss my parents.

On the whole, the boarding school experience was an enriching one. Although it ended my career as globetrotting ambassador in general, it taught me a lot. About myself more than anything else. I also learned that all Indians aren't nerds—many of them party and date ... they're actually pretty normal! (There's a laugh!)

It's only now that I've graduated from college that I feel like a relatively well-adjusted, functional adult. This is largely thanks to the fact that I've been in a steady, somewhat incredible relationship for two and a half years now (well, it's actually about a year and a half if you don't count the time spent apart on vacation). I've stopped worrying about many things, like my crooked teeth, my crooked fingers, and the fact that I talk too fast.

Of course, now that I've graduated, and NOT got my scholarship to Oxford, I feel like a retard. But I am working on that. As my sister once told me, sometimes life throws you this curve ball, and there's not much you can do. The real problem is when you feel that your entire life has been a curve ball, but I think I've left that stage behind me.

The key is not denying or dismissing your past, but accepting it. Your sanity depends on your moving on. We all make mistakes, and everyone's parents are human. Now that I can put things in perspective, I can see that my parents aren't the worst. They're not ogres ... they probably just had a nine-year bout of acute PMS or something. And although I do not appreciate their constant put-me-downs when I was growing up, it can't have been all that bad. I made it through, didn't I?

on being labelled a feminist

alankrita

I read *The Woman Destroyed* by Simone de Beauvoir. I can't sleep at night.

I watch *Mitra* and I think it the most wonderful film. The fact that the crew is predominantly female comes through.

In college and university I do research projects on women directors in commercial Hindi cinema and *Figuring Out Ally McBeal*. I do a radio programme on women artistes. I make a two-minute film on the aftermath of marital rape.

And only yesterday I produced a ten-minute live programme I had scripted on the anguish of being 'Draupadi.'

A few weeks ago I read about a socialite who married a man who was already married. His first wife was apparently very happy and comfortable with the entire situation. I refused to believe that was the truth. I spent two days agonizing about what she must be going through.

My friends call me a 'hardcore feminist.' But do I dare to define myself that way?

I do listen good-naturedly to jokes about women drivers, I laugh when people sit in my car and criticize the way I drive.

My schooling at an all-girls' school (Welham, Dehradun) and my graduation from an avowedly feminist college (Lady Shri Ram, New Delhi) are thrown at me as accusations by my male friends. I do react, but only jokingly. Because I detect a sense of grudging respect, or perhaps envy? Or is that just my imagination employing mechanisms of defence?

I strike the right feminist notes. 'Chairperson

not chairman,' I say. 'Cameraperson not cameraman,' I scream. And maybe I am heard.

I tell my mother that she has never stood up for her rights. She agrees. But she is stronger now. Grown strong through suffering and disease. Cancer-stricken and left to fend for the entire family. Whoever said it was easy being a woman?

My mother—also educated at Welham, LSR and later IIM, Ahmedabad—gave up a lucrative corporate job to follow my father into the wilds of Bihar. Of course it was out of choice. But what did she gain? She is left fighting her battles alone. My father is too bogged down by heart problems and career setbacks.

As for my maternal grandmother, she couldn't finish studying medicine. She had to get married. But she took up a course in beauty therapy and carved out a new career for herself. She traveled the world on her own. At the peak of her career she became a social worker. And later switched back to beauty therapy. She stayed away from my grandfather for ten years, in order to work and ensure a better education for her children.

What is her legacy?

And what is the legacy I have received?

In my own life I feel a strength that flows from my grandmother to my mother, then to me. We are fighting a battle for survival, for life. My sister, out of school and raring to go, is about to join this battle.

What legacy am I going to pass on to her?

I feel this flow of strength, tangible and pulsating in my being. Empowering. These bonds are deep.

I plan to make a documentary about my mother's struggle as a woman and as a cancer patient. At this stage my identity seems deeply entwined with my mother's. I need to deal with this entangled identity, I need to share our experience. I need to tell my mother's story and my own story. And sometimes they are the same story.

Three or four years ago a man on a scooter tried to molest me while I was driving. My mother was in the passenger seat beside me. I screamed. He fled. My mother couldn't stop him.

At the end of it all we are just women. And the eve-teasers have their way. But two weeks ago, as I was driving, a man in a Sumo began winking at me and making lecherous lip movements. I guess I'm stronger now. Because I just told him very calmly that I'll call the police. He drove off.

And then I wonder ...

Am I only paying lip service to the concept of feminism? In my own very real dilemmas, am I really able to stand up for myself?

Years later when I am married and my husband betrays me what am I going to do? And I think of the newspaper article and the woman with her five children living in the walled city, 'happy' to share her husband with another woman.

And I think of *The Woman Destroyed*. A middle-aged homemaker who comes to know of her husband's involvement with another woman. She is party to it and unable to take a stand. She feels alone and defeated, rejected and destroyed.

And what of Draupadi, betrayed by all her husbands?

Last year I went to shoot a documentary in Jaunsar Bawar in Garhwal. Here they worship the Pandavas and the women follow Draupadi's way of life, being married to two or more brothers. But the system remains patriarchal. On the woman falls the greatest burden of work as well as the task of satisfying all her husbands. How different is polygamy from polyandry? The woman never seems to win.

So is there really any hope for me?

And then I look at myself writing these words, this strange collection of random thoughts and incidents. There is hope yet.

Is there any one experience that defines the urban woman in me? I think not, I think the fact that I am a young educated urban Indian woman defines all my experiences.

I am almost twenty-three. An age when many young women get married. My friends have begun to get married. Arranged marriages and love marriages. Sometimes engagements are fixed with the girl having spent barely a few hours with her potential husband. I attend the wedding ceremony. I am excited. But the excitement often gives way to questions and fears and doubts. Is he the right guy for her? Will he keep her happy? Is she doing the right thing?

Everyone gets married. It's nothing new. But it is…

And then faint voices surface from my memory. 'These kinds of girls are fine for going out with, you know, they are girlfriend material. But one can't marry them.' 'Any girl who is twenty-three years old or more and not married is a reject from the marriage market.' Words spoken by young men like us. Did they mean these words?

Do they live by these concepts? Are they really hypocrites?

And what about me? Do I have double standards as well?

I have written over a thousand words. My sister quickly reads through what I have written. It's fine. But you haven't shown any emotion or explained why you work on the themes that you do. That is the essential question I am asking. Why do I choose to work on certain themes, why am I influenced by certain events?

Perhaps my friends are right and I am a 'hardcore feminist.' Do I shy away from this label? Am I proud of it? I don't know. It's just the way I am.

It is ironic that in both my research projects I deal with this issue. Tanuja Chandra did not want to be called feminist. Yet an analysis of her films yielded her as feminist to me. Watch *Dushman* and *Sangharsh*. Notice the women protagonists, the all-women self-sufficient families, the camera movements (very untypical of Bollywood, where the camera lingers over the heroine's body). And you will see what I mean.

The same goes for Ally McBeal. See her walking alone, working, independent and in search of true love. She is a feminist in her own right.

Yet she shies away from being termed an ardent feminist.

I hate the fact that we women have to worry about waxing our legs, threading our upper lips, pimples and dealing with our periods. The men really seem to have a better deal. But I still go through the routine ordeals of being a woman. Not waxing my legs is not a sign of feminism for me.

I drive alone at night. Without a mobile phone. I have been stranded at three o'clock in the morning. That was almost two years ago. But life carries on. And one can't live in the shadow of fear. I have a right to go where I want when I want and how I want. Just because I am a woman should my rights be different?

It's strange how our instinctive reactions betray us. I was driving home at about nine o'clock at night. The weather was lovely. Nizamuddin Bridge was buzzing with cars and I could feel the refreshing post-rain breeze. At the red light, the doors of the Maruti van next to me suddenly opened. My instinct was to put up the car windows and lock the door. I did exactly that. Only then did I dare take a look to see what was happening.

Nothing. The driver had gotten out to catch a bus while the passenger now sat in the driver's seat. Was I paranoid?

And what gives any random man the right to touch me, to look at me lecherously or to say something lewd because I happen to belong to the female sex? How much do we ignore? How often do we pretend not to have heard that stray remark, the whistles directed at us? How often do we desensitise ourselves to a man touching us when he shouldn't? But does it go away just because we pretend nothing has happened? They all say, 'Don't react. You'll be giving them attention. That is exactly what they want.' But are we not encouraging them each time we don't speak up? There is no clear course of action.

I met a friend of mine after very long. She plans to marry her boyfriend. 'Shall I change my surname?' she asks me. 'No,' I tell her, 'I wouldn't want to change my name.' I see her expression. And I know she will take her husband's surname. I have another bright idea. 'You can retain your original surname as your middle name and use your husband's surname.' This goes down better but she is still vague and won't commit herself. What's in a name after all? At least she is not changing her first name. Another friend of ours is changing even that.

So maybe it doesn't matter? But then what does?

When is it okay to give in?

When is it important to put your foot down? A soon-to-be bride asks her mother. 'What shall I do if my husband comes back home after work and asks me to get him a glass of water? Shall I get it or shall I tell him to help himself?' Or is it not an issue at all?

I yearn to make commercial feature films. Films about stories I feel a need to tell. I believe my perspective will be informed by the fact that I am a particular kind of woman, and that I am a woman at all. I don't necessarily want to be labeled a 'feminist' filmmaker. But I would like my films to be feminist in nature. Feminist in that that they explore the woman's point of view, feminist in that they are sensitive to the injustice of unequal rights and opportunities. Feminist in that they are conceived and created from a subjective position that is female in nature.

I have this strange gift for finding strains of feminism in the smallest details of life.

For feminism to me means the articulation of the woman's voice, or rather women's voices. Let women speak: in different strains, using different notes, different pitches ...

And let us speak so that we can hear ourselves. Let us speak so that we can hear each other. Let us also speak so that 'the others' can hear us.

Our voices are not one.

I will not become a feminist just because I claim to be one. I can also be feminist while avoiding the tag.

And then I wonder why people my age have such an aversion to being termed feminist. Why is 'feminism' associated with bra-burning, slogan raising and an all-out rampage against men?

As I see it, there was a time when women had to fight hard, tooth and nail for their place in the sun, and this struggle continues but it has taken a different form.

What people like us often seem to forget is that had it not been for the arduous battle fought by previous generations of feminists we would not have been where we are today. We would not enjoy the rights we do today. (And I know I sound like I have just read *Backlash*.)

I don't proclaim myself a feminist. But when I am called a feminist I feel a quiet sense of pride.

I am proud to be a woman. I am happy to be a woman.

But am I really feminist? Can I truly stand up for my rights?

I am not afraid of being called feminist. But so many like me are. People often told me, 'You scare men away.' I almost believed it. And just in the nick of time I didn't slide. I found someone who is not scared of me.

And then I saw all my lip service, theories and rhetoric falling to pieces. I think he just doesn't understand me. Most of the time he is completely insensitive to my needs. But deep down he is a nice guy. And I am an emotional sucker. I will not leave him. What does that make me?

Do I still have the right to call myself feminist? I cannot practice what I preach. And then I get the shivers. When I am married, what if my husband abuses me? Will I take it lying down? Will I put up a fight? Will I have the courage to walk out?

And suddenly I see myself like so many other women. Strong but still weak. Women who don't tell their stories. Women who pretend it's okay. Women who suffer within the four walls of their home.

And the personal does not become the political. And words don't translate into action. And what have I been propagating? And what I have been telling other women? And what high opinion had I of myself? And when the illusion is shattered I am just like all the others.

The situation is hypothetical. I have yet to be in an abusive relationship. I hope I will never be in one. But now the faith in my own steely strength and willpower is gone. It's not always black and white. Emotions colour situations grey.

I have spent so much time defining myself as a feminist that when I am strip myself of the tag who am I? What kind of woman am I?

shock of recognition

deveshe

We pulled up outside the gates of my apartment building. I peered at the front of my building and hastily placed my hand on my escort's. I didn't want him blowing the horn to wake the watchman and along with him the entire building. I was still quite drunk, I wasn't sure I could do it but I knew there was no other choice. There was a light on in my house so someone was awake. I climbed over the gate because it squeaked when it opened and

I didn't want anybody to realize what time I had come in. I took the steps up as well and opened the door very quietly. Seeing that whoever was in the bathroom was still in there I dashed across the drawing room on tiptoe, reached the safe zone of my bedroom, threw off my shoes and dived into bed in all my finery. My handbag was still on my shoulder. I woke up in the morning with a pounding, thumping hangover to show for the revelry of the night before. Putting on my nightclothes I went outside to get some water. I was surprised to meet my father; I'd thought he would be gone for the day. He smiled at me and said, 'I think we have mice. There was something scurrying about last night. Couldn't have been you. It was only five and you never get home before seven.' I was astounded by how 'cool' he seemed at that moment. It was too bad that I'd only just mastered the art of climbing the gate in a short skirt with dignity intact. It had taken a lot of practice.

Judging from my behavior when I was *young,* one would not have predicted the partying every night that makes my parents point out, wryly, how they seem to be running a hotel. Though not necessarily partying every night, I say partying with the express purpose of evoking the stereotypes associated with a 'party girl', i.e. sexually liberated, freethinking, open-minded, assertive even aggressive when necessary, often intoxicated, experimental, unafraid. Instead, when I was growing up (the past tense is part of the arrogance ascribed to my peer group) one would have imagined I was doomed to spend all my time in the library. I was the kid with her nose in a book who went down to play only because she'd been ordered to. I grew up reading a lot of Enid Blyton, and as I got older my reading material did not alter so very much in terms of its clear moral divisions. I graduated to reading the classics, with all their Good vs. Evil, three guesses as to who'll win, sometimes more depending on the intricacy of the plot. *Tess of the D'ubervilles*, *Pride and Prejudice* and *Vanity Fair* had a great impact on my mind, beautifully written, pulling my heart apart. There was a certain pleasure in living this morality vicariously. I was buying into it, because as a reader one is made to identify with the essentially 'good' character. The person you're supposed to identify with is always the protagonist, the girl who curbs her rebellious streak to settle down and resists her baser instincts even though it means getting screwed over by the bitch in the story. You're happy for the Elizabeths and Janes in the story, but at the same time you're worried because the character that seems more like you, all self-centered, ambitious, assertive, not a man-fixated pushover basically, is the one you see more of yourself in. The character that seems more real, instinctual, easier to be and infinitely more fascinating is also the one who always gets her just desserts in the end. I would sweat and swallow through to the ending of every book knowing in my heart which ending would be mapped out for me if I didn't conform. Then I would pick up another book hoping for a different ending, a more forgiving perspective but I can count on my fingers the books where I found this.

Here I am, sitting in a chrome and vinyl booth shielded somewhat from the flashing, probing, strobe lights. The loud music makes it difficult to have a conversation but easy to precipitate a somewhat intimate situation where my mouth verges on his ear. The haze of alcohol has settled on my brain and I'm a little stoned too. This makes me somewhat lethargic but I appear almost soft and pliable. I am assailed by a moment of highly avoidable self-reflexivity. I know he has a girlfriend.

I know she doesn't like the whole club scene thing. Here I am about to kiss him. I look down at my clothes—low-slung, fitting Levis, a cowl-necked crochet halter—and almost chuckle. He follows my gaze to my breasts, his heavy eyelids drooping over his very interesting brown, gray-flecked eyes. He leans towards me, I close my eyes. Before my mind surrenders to sensation I can't help but wonder which part I would be playing if this were a scene in a film? Would the audience shake their heads in disapproval as they stuffed popcorn in their mouths or would they mirror my inward smile of triumph? But I was in a good mood that evening, so I decided it would depend on whom the film was about, me or her (poor girlfriend in bed with her teddy bear) or him, even.

The colorful whirl I like to live my life in comes to a grinding halt and everything goes black and white. I sneak a glimpse at myself through the watchman's eyes as he opens the gate for me night after night as I bid goodbye to a different boy (does he think I'm a hooker?), or through the eyes of the girls in the train dressed in salwar kameez who were trying to embarrass me into buttoning my shirt a little higher but were discussing going to Aksa beach with their boyfriends, or my grandmother who has a scrapbook of newspaper clippings of girls who were sexually assaulted, beaten and so on, which she very solemnly makes me go through every Monday afternoon as I lie on the sofa recovering from the weekend. I see the shades of gray which make up the black and white picture, but do they? And if they don't, how does that make one of us inferior and the other superior? They're perfectly happy traversing their world with its clear divisions while I'm drifting around hoping the rainbow that livens up the gray sky will never fade away.

Why does it seem like I'm eternally doomed to skirt the edges? Being the one aware of not being the other? In a situation where I'm being bad with the awareness of only that and others where I'm being good or rather am forced into being good, all upset because I'd rather be bad but know it's not going to work in this instance. By bad I mean selfish, heartless, inconsiderate, opportunistic, undependable ... all the elements of future success and happiness. Then there are situations when I'm trying not to be judgmental because I'm of the opinion that those judging are the ones who have no other amusement or means to feel superior. I have to stop myself every now and then though, wipe that smirk off my face because I'm being too critical. Then there are times when I look across the room and see very clearly what somebody might be thinking. My instinct is to whip out the remote control in my bag and pause the scene, jump across the room and explain how it's not what they think, not entirely. I want to explain that I'm a nice person too, with feelings and thoughts and sensitivity. I believe 'true' liberation lies more in the awareness of being liberated than it does in the exploits of the liberated.

One of the compensations of leading a westernized lifestyle in India is that a lot of books have been written about the scenarios I like to color my experiences with. I acquired books like Herman Hesse's *Steppenwolf,* Jack Kerouac's *On the Road,* and *Dharma Bums,* Irvine Welsh's *Acid House* and *Trainspotting, The Great Gatsby* by F. Scott Fitzgerald and finally *Bridget Jones's Diary.* Reading continues to be an act of self-immersion. Like looking for a true image of myself in a room full of funhouse mirrors. I keep walking, glimpsing distorted versions of myself, from some of which I back away, while others seem like something I could become, and a few make me stop, absorbed, wishing that I could merge into them. Reading these books has been an experience of experience. It's been a welcome help to have some kind of reference point for what could be considered a nihilistic, hedonistic approach to life, when really I'm just trying to have fun and enjoy fully the freedom I am lucky enough to have been awarded.

I thrive on the fact that the world we inhabit is perpetually in a state of transition. It's sounds like a cliché (what are clichés but the truth too often reiterated), but sometimes I see things speeding up to the point where change occurs everywhere at lightning pace. For me, specifically, the defining moment was the switch from having just Doordarshan to having Cable TV. For my generation Cable TV came and changed how we felt about commitment and attention. Doordarshan had been all about going out of your way to watch something you weren't sure you liked but were forced to watch because there was no choice, at least none you were aware of. And then one day we were handed remotes with buttons 1–100—a whole level higher than the one or two we had had earlier. Commitment went out of the window when you found there was always something bigger, better and infinitely more entertaining if you kept switching the channel. Growing up was not so much growing older or gaining experience as it was a relaxing of social convention. School friends would barely admit to kissing and petting and now conversation centers on anal and same sex experiences (I know nativists and purists are weeping here). We evolved from stealing cigarettes and the occasional sip from daddy's bar to buying them from the corner paan-waala and asking for that drink. I envy people born a few years later because they take their liberty to drink, smoke, be sexually confident and opinionated as a given, as the social norm. They seem so much more relaxed about their liberation, so much more confident wielding it ... hence that much more liberated. I am somewhat sympathetic to those who were born a few years older than me who entrapped themselves in long-term monogamous relationships because that was the social norm then. But then I stop and remember that no matter how fluid and ever-changing our world has become, the one thing that persists are choices. I'm looking at the choices we've made, and at those others have made. We chose one path over another. Did I do the right thing? And more importantly will I ever gain a helpful moment of clarity? Even if I do who will benefit? I'm selfish enough to hope that I'm not offering myself up as a guinea pig for the next generation to use as a lab specimen. And then I recite to myself ... the magic mantra of survival ... 'Welcome to the here and now.' Thinking about anything beyond that or before it is an exercise in futility. You missed out for a second, now you have to catch up.

I wonder what is so different about our day and age that makes consequences seem like a fact only in fiction? When we decided that a heaven on Earth was a definite possibility did we factor in Hell? Will I be 'punished' in the not-so-distant future like the heroines of my heart from all the childhood books lying abandoned in my bookcase? I wish I could fast-forward to a few years ahead. What would be ideal would be to jump back to the present day as soon as I've seen enough of the imminent me to be reassured. That's something my not quite limitless imagination doesn't allow. But then I remind myself that these will be some of the best years of my life and I should not lose them in the haze of thinking too much. I should be out there crowding my senses, experiencing as many new things as possible ... trying everything at least once. This is a great excuse for sleeping on a park bench, smoking a chillum in Colaba with the homeless guys (who have very big chillums but some of the worst hash I've ever smoked), bungee jumping, skinny-dipping etc. Every so often I feel jaded, like there isn't as much to look forward to as I thought there would be. It comes and goes though. I'm aware that there'll come a day when being uninterested and cynical and uninspired may feel like more than a passing phase but I console myself with the thought that I can then absorb myself in the Herculean task of unwinding the tangled web that my memory will be by that time.

I'm walking down the street smiling to myself. Let everyone think I'm crazy! I look down at my hands and see there is sand still embedded in the gaps between my fingers. It glitters in the sunshine. Last night we were hanging out at a friend's house, drinking wine and watching a film when we started talking about how agreeable it would be to do the same on a beach instead. To watch the sea like it's a film while sipping wine. So we took a three-hour drive to the beach. On the way back the car broke down so some of us decided to take the ferry home. We had to squeeze in between the regular travelers, fisherwomen on the way to the market, schoolchildren and laborers on cycles. It was amusing to watch their amusement at our get-up and disheveled condition. Still in our party clothes we looked like battle-weary birds of paradise. We were obviously only just done with our night while their morning was beginning. Our spectators laughed at us and nudged each other as they stared. We laughed at the fact that they found us so amusing. I almost fell into the sea while getting off the rickety boat that was at the mercy of the sea and wind. I wouldn't have minded too much ... everybody would have laughed some more and then we'd all have gone our separate routes.

My spine tingles with excitement and I can barely keep still when presented with the opportunity to experience something I haven't done before. But at the same time I must admit that the freedom I am given comes together with the fact that I have the freedom to choose. I can choose to say no and it doesn't mean I'm less open to new experiences (the ultimate slur). I mention this simply because it took me a while to realize these particular words of wisdom ... that being liberated doesn't mean I have to go out all the time, party till dawn every day and say yes to whatever is on offer. The sixties and seventies were all about that and I think we might have learnt that lesson. I'm given the opportunity because I'm somewhat responsible or appear to be. I would probably be placed under house arrest if my parents saw (too many) track marks on my arm. And every now and then I am taken aside and lectured on my 'wasted' existence but I think there is no better place than Big Bad Bombay City to lead a wasted existence that might just lead to something fruitful. There is a seething subculture in this city that's big enough to maintain a level of anonymity and small enough to let you to get to know all the intriguing characters floating around. This is exciting because hopefully some have the power and drive to do innovative things later in life. Because with this sense of liberation comes a sense of awareness that you don't have to conform to the stereotypes of what one should and shouldn't hope to achieve. You can fall in love, get married and have kids and have a career and still have a life, or so the generation that wants to have its cake and eat it too would like to believe.

I'm standing at the door of my house, kissing my mother goodbye and trying to tell her my plans for the night over the impatient horn-blowing of my friends. I make a run for the elevator but can't help hearing the concern tingeing her voice as she tells me to get back early. I smile at how predictable it all is. What about my mother? Where does she stand in all this? What effect does she have on my confused psyche? What does she hope to achieve through it? She once asked me if I experienced everything now what I would do later. That's a thought that does worry me. But then maybe I'll start reading again or do social work. Will I still be mentally alert or will my edges be dulled from too much rubbing?

Sometimes she tells me stories about going to Blow Up and partying until dawn, brimming over with amphetamines; about midnight coffee runs, wearing midriff-exposing tops and low-slung skirts with slits up to her thighs; about her mother catching a boyfriend sneaking out of her bedroom at 3 a.m.; and I can't help but cringe at how alike we are. The only real difference seems to lie in our age and the fact that where her mother expressed complete disapproval, mine exhibits only concern because she sees me making the same mistakes. It's not like I had my freedom handed to me on a platter, I have to earn it by proving myself responsible enough to merit it. I'm unsure sometimes as to whom it was harder for, my grandmother or my mother? My grandmother who had to deal with knowing that her precious child was breaking all the social norms and would be frowned upon by society, or my mother who can see history repeating itself.

soul searching

phoenix

2004

16th July, 12:30 am

Where do I picture myself ten years from now?

I would be 32 years old, a well-known writer in an extraordinary profession. I would be happily married to a brilliant man with a beautiful child.

I would be serene.

And now let's talk about where I am right now. I am unwell. I am in a bad relationship. My life feels like it is going nowhere. I wake up each day with a class to attend. I spend time with 'him' and always come home feeling like nothing, constantly disappointed about something. Forever feeling unloved and unwanted. Even though I tell myself not to suffer that way, I always seem to feel lost.

Have I forgotten who I am?

I know I will discover myself. I believe I am a survivor and I will fight to hang in there.

Life is very brutal right now. Everything seems to be conspiring against me.

But slowly I want to achieve, I want to see the world, I want to discover. I want to live far away from here. I want to some day stumble upon me.

I don't want to be afraid anymore. I want to liberate myself from the burden I have carried in my soul so that I can live my life the way I was intended to.

I want to be all I wished to be, whether a salsa dancer, a killer-whale–trainer, or someone working with chimps.

I want to do it all and be that girl who walks into a room and makes it come alive. So when you look into my eyes, you see me, you too believe that I am special…

1991
26th June

What is Death?

Who is God?

And finally is it all fair?

Why do these things happen? And this is where it all began…

She told me about her dream the night before. She was in a temple and had seen a man covered in mud. He was holding out his hand to her. He had told her that he had come to take away her pain. She told me he was Shiva who was going to create a painless life for her. But I didn't want to hear about anything that would take her away

from me. She was a fighter, not the person who
had given up hope she was pretending to be.

Later that day someone came and told me
she was asking for me. My heart was racing.

Had the time come?

Had she given up?

As I walked into that room I froze. This was not
her. It was someone who looked like her lying
there lifeless. I didn't even get to say goodbye.
I felt cheated! How could she leave me in
this big bad world all alone?

How am I supposed to go on?

I am only a child...

She was my all and without her I am lost.

She was my definition of perfection,

She was my creator,

She was my mother.

My mother was going teach me to be
a good person. She was someone who when
she saw caged birds would make me buy
them and set them free. She told me that
birds didn't belong in cages, they

belonged to the sky. She always told me to
treat everything in life, animal or
human, with respect.

Am I growing up too fast?

Am I seeing too much too soon?

I am not ready to deal with all of this.
I blamed God for stealing my childhood. I
am too busy fighting the world. I
want to cry for her.

The man covered in mud has won.
My mother left my hand and took his. For me
he was not the creator but the destroyer.
He took her away from me.
And that was the day
I lost my faith and
started to fight God!!

I don't believe in love. I don't want
to get attached to anyone or
anything again. I feel if
I do then they would also
leave me alone
like she did.

Love is a bad thing...

1994
7th April

He has come...

I was walking back from class when I saw him, and for the first time in a very long time my heart smiled.

Who is he?

I had never seen him before. By chance or destiny, whatever you want to call it, he managed to take away my pain. We were happy, I was happy. I felt alive again. Life didn't seem all that bad, there was still hope.

It was the first time I fell in love. Everything around me appeared blissful. I started sharing my heart bit by bit with him. I wanted to love him without end. I was precious to him.

I had been so very lonely and to find someone who wanted only to love me made me sparkle. I had decided to give him my innocence without even understanding the depth of its value, and later discovered this would leave a stain on me forever. An injury I could never forget.

I know it was too early to understand the value of what I gave him. But I believed in him. He would never hurt me. He said he loved me. I entrusted myself to him. I would have given my life for him. I just wanted to make him happy.

And then came the storm. My father found out I had been involved physically with him. My world lost the warm rays of the sun and became dark. It was all a blur for the next few months. I was called names in school. To the point where I had people calling me up to ask what I would name my child. People who didn't even know me knew who I was. The girl who had had sex at the age of fourteen. I had not a place in the world to hide. At home I was treated with hate and disgust and in school I was treated like an untouchable. I didn't understand why, why people would be so unkind.

My father never forgave me after that day. And I guess I never forgave myself. I blamed myself for all the pain around me. Life was all about the next person attacking my existence and I would cry.

I have never seen such anger and such ruthless
attacks on my soul as I did at fourteen.
Unaware of how to stand up for myself.
Not knowing how to deal with such pain.
And the worst was being alone through it all.

My happy little world started fading. I was so
terrified but I got my strength from his love.
I knew he'd never leave me, he loved me
too much. He believed in us, like I believed
in us. And I was not going to lose another
I loved so dearly again. I was going to
fight with all I had for my love,
but then I saw.

He let go of my hand right in the middle of the
storm. I saw what I didn't want to admit I had
seen. He gave me up and let the storm devour
me. My world was disappearing and there was
nothing I could do to save it.

Did I want to save it?

My heart broke into so many pieces that even if
I wanted I couldn't find them…
he destroyed my spirit,
He cheated me,
He lied.

Everything I thought I had known was untrue,
this was not the love he had promised. I felt
like an object being tossed away when
things got difficult. I am not precious
to him. The one he would
never let go of...

1994
4th September

From this day I swear I will never let anyone
near my heart. I will not trust again. I believe all
promises are made just for the moment
and then forgotten...

I am broken and defeated,
I am lost in the chaos...

1995
5th July

I have decided not to live life and to let life live
me. People come and go. I believe I am
an object. No one can love me, for if they
could the two people I had loved would
not have left me and they did. The
whole world has the right to treat
me as a passing thought.

My feelings and emotions don't count, I am just a face, a body, not a person but an object with no wants, no feelings. No rights for I don't deserve anything.

I must have done something terrible to deserve all this pain. Should I just fall in love with pain? The ever-faithful pain.

It is a drug without which I am lost. I look for pain, and I know that I am alive...

1998
3rd June

Years have gone by and so have people and then in walked the boy next door.

He is my best friend. He didn't make me run as the ones before had. He made me stop, gaze and smile. And then I thought I could see a little light in my sky. The darkness was lifting and there was light.

He is very good to me. He even takes care of me.

Is there something wrong with him?

Doesn't he see the girl the world sees?

Things are going well and everyone seems happy.

What's wrong?

Why doesn't he leave me?
I am still addicted to my pain...

2000
19th July

I have started panicking. I am scared
of happiness and I refuse to acknowledge it.
I am not ready to let go of my pain. He will
walk away and I will be back in my gap in the
darkness, which is my own. The only thing I
recognize, the only form of comfort I know.
I am safe in my shell of pain. Alone...

2002
2nd August

My agonizing school life is finally over and I'm
applying to colleges for courses,
they are meaningless to me
but they make my father happy.

I am studying in India for a year as they have
promised to send me away next year. I work
part-time for an advertising firm
but it all seems pointless to me.

I seem to be going deeper into emptiness.

For the first time I did exactly what they
wanted. Got good grades for that
year and towards the end of my
semester I started applying
to colleges abroad.

One day they told me they couldn't send me
away as I hadn't got a scholarship.

I felt the same piercing pain on hearing their
words. I felt cheated. Again...

2002
25th November

I have already been here. This has all happened
before so why is it happening
again? This time I don't
want to fight.

I have found a substance, which helps me
slip out of reality. The haze
makes everything
numb.

I can't see,

I can't feel,

I don't want to be.

2002
15th December

The numbness has taken over. I am escaping.
The real world is left behind. And that's where
I met him. Another 'him.' In my world of
emptiness he was something that flirted
with my fears. I let myself go. I am
accustomed to flowing like a river,
but this path will not lead to the
sea. I know it and I feel it but my
defeated spirit cannot guide me.
I have let go of everything
that is dear to me.
I let him guide me out of my turmoil into his
darkness...

2004
6th January, 4:15 am

I know that we are connected. I read
somewhere, 'Life is insane, but you should
choose your insanity wisely.'
Are you the insanity I chose?
Why is it so hard for two people who love each
other to get along?

Why is the chemistry so strong that it keeps
blowing up in our face?

I have felt physical pain and have put you
through an emotional storm, but after every
storm isn't there a rainbow?

Experiences make one wiser ... or do they open
channels that weren't there earlier to prepare
us for more heading our way?

My pain captivates me. I find it safer to be
there than to find a way out and face something
I am not ready for. I was told that we all
choose the lives we want before we
come into this world.

So am I to take it for granted that I will make it
through only because I have chosen to
experience it?

Or do I listen to that twinkling voice inside,
telling me I have to hold on, even when there's
something stabbing my heart and
hurting me terribly?

Do I follow that twinkle or the old cliché?

How do I decide?

Who makes the rules?

Who says what's right and what's wrong?

Don't we make the rules for ourselves and doesn't everyone deserve forgiveness?

I can't breathe with all these questions in my head to which I do have answers but do I have the strength to stand by my soul?

I learned a long time ago that life is short. Forgive and forget, tell someone how you feel because soon they may not be around to play the silly little games we all play. I always believed in that perfect love which I am yet to find...

2004

27th January, 1:28 am

Human beings are strange creatures. Sometimes so predictable and sometimes you wonder whether we all came from the same place or God knows where?

It's so easy to break my spirit just because you didn't feel like accepting it, and when I decide to walk away you suddenly realize that I was the one thing that completed you.

Everything has so many reasons and meanings. I suddenly feel like my head is spinning

and my world is whirling. I just know that I
need to have time with myself, to understand
myself better as I am in no position to
make decisions that might just end
up sending my wavering world
off its orbit into
another dimension.

Why are you making me so unsure of myself?

Why do you lie to me about everything, and
when I catch you, deny it?

Why are you playing games with my mind?

Why don't I just let you go???

On one hand I have my heart and on the other
I have my soul and I know they both have been
traumatized to a point where maybe only
I can fix them, not love, not
friendship but me...

2004

28th January, 8:30 pm

When do I say enough and move forward?

I think it's when even though it's easier to hold
onto something or someone who's been a
major part of my life for a very long

time, I can't breathe when I am with him any
more, I feel like something terrible is going to
happen when he is just being himself. I sit by
his side, and look away and picture myself
running on a beach, I am free, my spirit is
smiling and then I turn my face and reality
strikes. The beach might be waiting
but I need my closure.

What am I so afraid of?

I can see the peaks in the distance. I can see the
ocean, and it all awaits me. But I need to take
the strides towards it. I need to walk forward
without any baggage. But what if my
baggage has become a part of me?

How do I let go of it?

When in return he believes I belong to him.
How do I convince someone who believes I am
the one for him that I believe he
isn't the one for me?

I know I will be fine without him. I have
everything to gain, but he won't let me go. He
believes I'm the one who's going to fight his
demons for him, but what about
my demons?

Who's going to fight mine if I am fighting his?

Maybe he's right. Maybe I am the one for him.

A relationship, what is it all about?

I thought when you are with someone, they are
supposed to make you happy.

Then why does this feel all wrong?

Do you wound the one person you proclaim
to love entirely and leave them
feeling absolutely helpless?

Is that love?

2004
9th February, 1:07 am

Sometimes I just want to live without any
significance, with no foundation, just the
fact that I wake up, get through the day
somehow, and go to sleep. The same
pattern day after day and I get so
caught up in that pattern
that I take it for
life itself.

It has taken me very long to see things in a different light and even longer to change these patterns. I am still trying to change.

I know what's right. It's within me. It's just that I close myself off and let things happen to me, as it's easier to blame the world than to blame myself. But the truth is within me. I know sometimes my good and bad deeds go unrecognized. Some people call it luck.

But what is it really?

Is there something out there watching me and giving me chances to maybe fix things? And sometimes things happen to me to make me realize that life is not to be taken lightly…

2004
16th March, 2:50 am

What happens when I am standing in front of those two doors?

Both have light shining behind them. Both take me to completely different places.

It's just the music and me. Everything else is forgotten. I am eternity, I am the universe, I am alone and that has no meaning.

In one blink I am scribbling thoughts down and listening to sounds that drag me towards them. Even though I don't understand or know what I am being pulled towards, I know it's strong. I am being held with such force that I can barely breathe.

If it lets go of me, I would wither away like a lotus in a desert.

Life is changing at this very moment and I feel it in every sign of my body that I am both scared and excited.

There is something stronger out there and right now it has me mesmerized. Is it trying to show me something?

These words that are flowing through me at this moment, are they mine?

I know that I am not lost. And when I close my eyes all I hear is the sound of a bird and I picture myself under a waterfall, and I know that I am free. My spirit is ready to endure what lies ahead in my path...

2004

20th March, 5:30 am

Could there come a time in my life that shakes my entire life and makes it meaningless?

Could my soul come to a point when it tells me
that I am insane?

That everything I feel isn't real, all that I saw
didn't happen, what I said wasn't heard!

Could people and circumstances really
twist the truth?

Turn my emotions against me?

Is it so easy to be misunderstood?

How do I save myself from me?

Am I crazy? Have I become delusional,
can nobody hear me?

I find myself in a state of hysteria. I have felt so
much pain and injustice. I have said and done
things I didn't think I was capable of.
I have lost.

I find myself being stripped of my feelings, my
self-esteem and pride. I have not the thinnest
sheet to cover myself. I feel unprotected, with
no shield or a sword, in the middle of a war
between my reality and people twisting my
actions and emotions against me.
Every action, every word misunderstood. There
is nothing I can do to prove my innocence.
I have been made the murderer

when I feel like I was the one dying.
Why am I being put through so many tests and agony?

Why can't I live a peaceful life?

Why does my world always have to be in a state of maximum destruction?
At this point I find myself bewildered, as I feel it can't really be happening, when it is.

Is it me?

Am I crazy?

Have I created all of this???

2004
20th March, 7:45 pm

Is it finally time to wake up?

Is it time to give up this never-ending battle, whose only outcome is pain?

Should I accept defeat?
I couldn't change you, so I became you, and in the process of trying to find you, I vanished.
I have no ground to stand on as I have misplaced my soul. Standing behind you, I sank deeper and deeper into quicksand without realizing I was in it too. There is no one

standing behind me to pull me out.

Is it time to save you and destroy me?

I thought all I would get was love. But all I got back were lies, injustice and abuse.

Why would you abuse me and make me out to be someone I'm not?

Why would you look me in the eye and make me out to be a liar when you lied?

When you are the one being treacherous?

I have shared my soul with you. I have taken you to the happiest and saddest places in my heart.

Doesn't that add up to something?

I don't even feel like a person anymore. I have been drained of everything I ever believed in.

Would you deliberately destroy my spirit?

Would you take my soul and squeeze it out of existence?

2004
7th April, 8:40 pm

I feel like a new phase is starting. I feel different. Something in me is growing up. I am learning to let go slowly. I finally want to get up. I think I am ready for this big bad world. I think it is time to deal with my pain the right way. No more overcrowding. It's all about accepting, and once you accept life it will accept you.

I will move forward and I am moving. Not wishing and not hoping, but finally free...

2004

21st April, 2:05 am

I woke up today with a smile. I had a magnificent dream. It's like a completely new me. I feel beautiful. I am glowing. My spirit and soul are sparkling like the sun. I feel illuminated. I think I could fly. My inner strength is mounting. My spirit is smiling. It's a fantastic Sunday. This is how I want to feel everyday.

I am ecstatic as I see my life unfold. I have started my journey and as I travel I don't know where the path is leading me, which is (now, at last) fine, for the thirst in me to discover is unquenchable.

It's a glorious world. I want to explore it. My life has real meaning. It is of consequence.

I have finally aimed for my spot between stars and I will find my place. The journey has begun; as I don't need any man to complete me, I know I am already complete...

the abyss and mulligatawny soup

mukulika

Introduction: Day and Night

'The Abyss' celebrates the whimsical, bohemian Night and the touch of despair and listlessness among bats, ravens and other nocturnal creatures reveling in life and desire. The Night, as it unravels its darkness, descends into a haunting spiral of blankness and uncertainty. In the drum and bass of my existence, the drumbeat and the bass have withered into fragments of sound—incoherent and wafting on fancies without anchor. Sounds submerge my mind softly in twilight dust and sadness. I feel a sense of longing and loss, without quite understanding what I have lost and what I long for.

'Mulligatawny Soup' is Day—luminous and intense, driven by an inner conflict that besieges my soul. Of feeling disconnected from India, and yet tied to it by an umbilical cord. Of being Indian and yet not quite in sync with India. Of yearning to escape but not knowing the how or where of escape. Of finding diversions in work, dance, hedonism and occasionally in the art of living itself. Of allowing ivory tower fantasies to consume my realities. And of not being sure where home really is.

There are sporadic, tragi-comic moments of living as a mannequin, trying out theatrical Wilde poses against a leering shop window. Of being attacked by an alien mind, fighting invaders on a barren landscape. Of living my days and nights with a joie de vivre, a nonchalance that only afflicts the truly despondent and the truly desperate.

Almost like a Greek farce, my Day and Night marry and live unhappily ever after. This could be a Bollywood hit. Now if only A.R. Rahman would compose the music. Because after all, who needs a script.

The Abyss

Purgatory is a crowded discotheque wearing a tired smile. Neon lights blaze amidst flashing faces and loud raucous music. A wintry night. The usual masks of lust, longing, hope and an occasional glimmer of romance pass me by as I continue my endless quest for excitement in a dungeon identified with pleasure.

I realize I am bored with hedonism. Especially when it has no meaning. For me.

Ironically, I also recognize that I speak the language, the pseudo-babble of Deepak Chopra, the mastermind salesman of soul-food. Even so, my thoughts wander as I sip my margharita, my elixir of happiness and my visa to Purgatory. My happiness can be measured by tall margharitas, vacant conversations and empty moments. Monotony lurks guerrilla style. It has been waiting a long while to make its terror attack on me. Me with my claim to having never been bored in my life. Me who's been dancing on my feet ever since I can remember, and laughing my smile which shines in my eyes.

My earliest memory of happiness is dashing down the hills of Kathmandu with my mother and dancing with the swaying trees. I was blooming with hope and energy. My mother who struggled with her own demons to make my life happy. Kathmandu was a monumental effort to bring 'us' together—my father, my brother and myself. My father spent most of his time in the casino—despite substantial monetary losses, it offered a better refuge than we did. My mother made the holiday happen anyway. In a sense she has made it happen all her life for us. It is a burden she wears lightly.

Despair struck when I was least expecting it. With adolescence came the ugliness of growing years and the haze of teenage existence. When I finally had the courage to embrace reality, I realized that reality was not quite ready to embrace me, whimsical and different. And though I have fought battles with myself time and again, my desert rose now beckons. I can no longer shy away even if it turns out to be just another mirage.

I am bored with the struggle to prove my worth and to make my contribution to this productive world. To jump hoop after hoop in a ceaseless effort to parade my ability, like a compliant dog obeying its master. To sing in chorus with this capitalist world of ants, rushing always, in time to a crescendo of progress chants. Slogans ramble in my head. *India Shining*. GDP that has progressively grown, a middle class well-fed on prosperity, roads that gleam with better, faster cars. And the holy seer by the roadside has more visitors and more offerings.

I leave the struggle to the worthy who have a Quest, to Seekers of Fame, Wealth, Beauty, Power and Happiness Within. Or alternately, to the insecure, those who give in to the underworld rats of greed, jealousy, ambition, which scamper faster than any other.

I let the waves of my life wash over me and sweep me away to something else … something better, something new. I occasionally wonder whether I frittered my brain and soul away or whether my sense of being, and my purpose for living has been stolen from me by mysterious djinns. Now I am just driftwood without even the ability to flow with the tide. I am driftwood caught by the wayside rock trying to ascertain the course of the tide, the meaning of the river.

I think I tried too hard. The fable of King Bruce and his spider just didn't work for me.

I have been 'different' for as long as I can remember—my creativity lies submerged in a champagne bubble in my soul. However, I have nothing to show for my difference—I am a lawyer by day, a dancer in dreams and a social butterfly by night, sated by my midnight choreographies. I am acutely aware that we are all different. Before night ends, I want to revel in my 'difference', not bury it in a hidden corner. My ambitions change course mid-way—no longer just a safe existence of happily ever after with children to show for it, a steady job with a substantial income and a house over my head. My ambitions soar away from existence itself—into abstract algebra in dazzling choreography and haunting prose. I am ready to be swept away by my river of dreams before it is swallowed up by the sea of humanity.

I drink my margharita in a gulp of gay self-abandon (well-simulated) and watch the actors. Tonight, my acting is a bit wanting—even I am not convinced. The noise drowns out my mind's murmurs.

I try to catch a ray of neon light as it flashes past me, onto half-seen faces and bodies and swallow my sense of disillusionment. I remind myself that I am in search for witless prey to purge this disillusionment. But I am not hungry for prey. Tonight is a night for nothing at all, for drifting on waters of Wagnerian despair, chugged along by my ever-faithful Margharita.

Boredom, I am reminded constantly, is a state of mind. A simple equation: boredom = a state of mind. But one I cannot quite work out. My mind is always in a state—in fact, in fractured states and never silent of its 'states of being.' It has been accosted by too many states, too many upheavals of imagined and real worlds, and has worn too many badges to be entirely convinced.

Boredom is a reminder, a faint memory of disapproval and discontent worn on so many faces that they merge into one. Of that wry smile on my teacher's face as I earnestly try to answer a question on the chemical properties of methane. Of being unable to tie my shoelace. Of the wall between civilization and me. Of stumbling incoherently in my final dance examination in Kathak. Of being uncertain. Of smiling at nothing at all. Of seeing more than there is. Of hearing a different beat and yet never mustering the courage to follow it. Of faltering before I take a step.

It is the writing on the wall that I cannot quite decipher. A feeling of defeat and a merger and acquisition of my companies of Disillusionment and Insecurity.

My existence is a mirage, swaying to the heady mix of margharitas, neon lights and disco rhythms.

Boredom is also my mask, my shield of being above everything and nothing all at once. I wear my enchanted smile lightly. It is my smile of winter that keeps me warm.

The music continues ... Purgatory hums my song but never hears my cry.

Mulligatawny Soup

These are days of biryani accompanied by Scotch whisky and rioja. Of dressing down at social-climbing charity events. Of wallflower homemakers flirting outrageously with fame. Of Hinglish, and ethnic beaded kurtis worn with slim cigarette pants and pencil stilettos. Of buying *Cosmopolitan* and *The Economist* together. Of bhangra aerobics and the Atkins diet straddling each other in the war against obesity. Of dosa diners, McDonalds' aloo tikki burgers and golguppa vodka shots. Of yoga spirituality being marketed aggressively by multinationals.

It is an age of multiple roles—dedicated professional with monochrome ambitions; secular activist; Bohemian Artiste breaking tradition and surging forth on waves of creativity; nocturnal Barbie with no clue about anything, particularly politics and cricket; Dutiful Daughter; Convent Educated Girl filling matrimonial columns; Rebel with and without a cause.

Of breaking boundaries within and without.

Of Vajpayee touting India–Pakistan friendship and promoting Modi's vitriolic crusade against the minority. Of attempting to understand where the RSS/VHP are coming from and failing miserably. Of wondering why Bajrang Dal activists are driven to blacken a young man's face when he gives his girlfriend a Valentine's Day card in celebration of love. Love is apparently a dirty word in this populous country.

Of hypocrisy being tailored so delicately on the political sleeve that it is visible, but not striking.

Of the balancing act—the precarious perch between Western 'progress' and 'going back to our roots.' Being modern, cosmopolitan and liberal in one avatar and superstitious and traditional in the other. Of breaking free of the confines of patriarchal relationships and laughing sycophantically at sexist jokes at the workplace.

It is the story of those of us caught in between—between ourselves and society, between gay bohemia and convention, between faith and religion, between India's past and its present, between life and living, between thinking straight and spiraling in circles, between sanity and delusion, dreams and fantasy. It is the story of those of us caught between the choices we make.

En route to work, I listen to Arabic music ... my remote connector to the Muslim world and Islam—an Islam celebrating life, love and music. A floating Sufi philosophy in music that pours into my soul. An Islam I relate to. On my way back from work, I make my peace with Christianity by saying my prayers to Jesus and occasionally loving my neighbour. My understanding of Hinduism is limited to the belief that it is all-embracing rather than exclusionary. I wear my faith close to my heart, it is religion that I am irreverent to.

Living in a country whose USP may be only that it is the second largest democracy in the world, I find myself fascinated by the rhetoric of our right-wing government as it speaks the language of hatred in the name of religion, and points its finger at outsiders within, who do not belong to Mother India.

I look at myself, and realize that in my fractured, very mongrel identity—half Muslim and half Christian by birth (if halves exist in religion), half Keralite, one-quarter Bihari and one-quarter Kashmiri (and at heart really quite a Bengali)—makes me the sum of too many parts. It means I do not quite belong in the homogenous world that the BJP sees as India ... pure, white and simple. That their philosophy of India is crucially at odds with mine—in its black and white definition of good versus evil, in its belief in the exclusion of the electorally inconsequential, whether the religious minorities, or the secular elite (who add up to a miniscule metropolitan amoeba—hardly fit for electoral compromise) or foreign educated Indians with 'phoren' ideas, or anyone who does not fit their view of the world from their chariot of *ram rajya*.

I watch as Vajpayee deftly embraces the slogan 'India Shining', pats the BJP on the back for everything under the Indian sun, and charms all of us into believing in the BJP, 'the party that has offered India stability.' After all, the image influences our perception of reality, and as mirror images go, this is a remarkable optical illusion created by hard sell and brand imaging. I watch as he slowly but surely moves the camera away from Modi's excesses and the terror rule imposed in Gujarat on all minorities; from the communalism spreading like continuous see thing wildfire through this country; from isolated but frequent cases of the suppression of freedom in secessionist movements in the North and in the North-east; from the rampant corruption in this country that once embraced glory, regal splendour and aesthetic sensitivity.

India is more than the sum of its parts. More than the luxurous decadence of the past that the British stole. It is more than Bollywood songs that cross creed and class. It is more than urban and rural art and culture. It is more than the cows on the street which get more respect than starving urchins. It is more than the corrupt policeman taking bribes from the motorcyclist and truck driver but never from the rich man in his convertible. It is more than the roadside Romeo and the greasy, sleazy businessman making a pass. It is more than the injustice of waiting, more than the grief of the past, more than the confusion of today. It is more than the streets of shame and prostitution, and it is more than the spiritual nirvana that the world's celebrities come in quest of. More than the urban legend of India Shining. More than the guilt of the few who live in ivory towers and let their thought meander towards the poor between sips of Zinfandel. More than the smiles of ragpickers as they are fed by the local dhaba on Eid. More than the glamour of Bombay dreams and the inanity of celebrity existence. It is more than the family feuds that show the dirt underneath the richest tapestries. More than the contrast between commercial cinema and environmentally sensitive films. Between Page 3 and the Editorial Page. It is so much more than me in my debate with myself on my Indianness.

India allows me to be. To be angry. To be lost. To be confused. To be grief-stricken. To have the luxury of floating on waves of emptiness as the world moves on busily around me. To find my own tune against the deafening monotone of everyday existence.

India makes a mockery of my despair by wreaking havoc on those around me.

India taunts me with its ever-changing face, with its dynamic turns, with its ability to adapt and move ever so gracefully like a sinewy snake meandering on in the desert.

And I breathe easy despite everything—even as I do not quite fit in, do not quite understand the India I live in. It gives me the freedom to explore myself against its own powerful landscape.

I ride gently on the wave of disillusion, my discontent not engaging enough to disturb the peace of my coffee break entirely but still somehow nagging and persistent. Like a bird on a wire, I look up at the sky for enlightenment, and instead find two sparrows twittering in excitement as they follow each other across the twilight horizon. I smile at myself. While these sparrows have found their escape—saving themselves from the suffering of inanities that besiege and torment the mind just by being incapable of thought—my mind surfs against the tidal waves of despair. It is almost as if I have finally awakened from a blissful sleep of ignorance and naiveté and cannot find my way back. I stay awake dreamless. And raging. And against what, I cannot quite fathom. Which enrages me further. This is a fine perch to be on.

the howling

anonymous

We all live our lives in this continual, ever-changing pretence. We like to believe that 'culture' is a word coined by India. And yet we happily turn our faces from that most uncultured of situations: the enormous abuse that women in this country face.

We like to believe our gender relations are as good they can be. We claim that women are given more respect in this country than anywhere else. As a consequence, if they lose out on a bit of equality, it's nothing much. We're only ready for change that we can predict. We're only ready for change that has already been made. We refuse to challenge the problem, because its magnitude scares us. For us, ignorance is bliss.

Let us all pause ...

Look at that girl who smiles at you in the market. Look at that woman walking with her child, look at that girl you just met in a night club, look at that girl at the crossing, begging for a rupee, look at your sister ... or even your best friend ... they all might have a story to tell ... look at me ...

I am a girl ...

In 1997, I was molested by my uncle. I had a high temperature and could barely move. My brother, uncle and I were the only ones at home. The volume of the TV seemed to break through, pounding, into my head. I couldn't bring myself to get up so I just lay there waiting for the pain to go. It was when my brother left the room that it happened. I had been complaining of pain, so my uncle asked me if I wanted my shoulders pressed. A little reluctant, I said yes, hoping for some relief from the pain. Pressing my shoulders, he slowly slipped his hands down into my clothes and started fondling me. I was not so much sick and unable to move as shocked and unable to react. I didn't know whether what was happening was right or wrong. 'I can only do this with you, other people won't understand', he said.

With a little difficulty I moved his hands away from my body. As I was walking out of the room I knew he was saying something, but all I could hear was my heartbeat and all I could feel was sweat dripping down my thighs.

I was sixteen then. I had never liked my uncle and now I knew why ... he had done this before; when I was younger. It had just never registered, I guess. These were always 'hush-hush' things and were just not talked about. I don't know who had taught me that but I had learned it anyway. I never felt like the victim. Instead, I felt like I had done something bad.

Later that evening, I gathered my courage and told my parents. All they did was question him on the phone. Nothing ever really happened. He still comes over to our house.

I am a woman ...

Early 1999, I lost my virginity. I was drunk. He was a few years older than I. We had been seeing each other for just a couple of months.

I'm not sure, but for most girls, I think, losing their virginity is a big deal. Rather, how one loses it is a big deal. Well, that's exactly what happened to me. I lost my virginity. Not willingly, not because I wanted to. I simply couldn't push him away. He was stronger than I was … I was drunk. I tried pushing him, I hit, I punched. I didn't scream. I don't know why I didn't scream, considering that's the first thing one does when one's physical space is violated. I guess I didn't have any energy left. I just didn't scream. It's funny how all these little things come back to me now. 'It's hurting me!'—I remember saying that, and not just once. Almost as though I was chanting, hoping that it would touch his conscience somewhere and that he would stop. But this is only an afterthought. Right then, all I knew was that I didn't want it to happen.

I didn't tell my parents. I didn't tell anyone. We kept seeing each other for about three months after that. When I brought it up with him, he told me I was being stupid and childish. I believed him.

I had been raped. Or as some might say, I had been involved in sexual intercourse against my will.

I, now, am a woman. I had learned what physical abuse was and I had learned how to keep my mouth shut about it. You see, this has somehow become the definition of the Indian woman. It is almost as though it is her duty to understand that physical abuse will be a part of her life in some form or degree. And it is most certainly her duty not to speak about it. At the same time it is her duty to be a perfect daughter, a perfect mother, a perfect worker and above all, a perfect wife.

Well, I became a woman that night. And I wasn't eighteen yet.

I am a person

I was born in the early 1980s. My parents wanted a girl. In fact, they had been wanting one for quite some time. I'm sure that even before I was born they must've decided what I would be when I grew up, as most parents do. But in their dreams and aspirations for me, I wonder if they had ever paused to think whether I would be allowed to be what I actually am: a girl.

Today my femininity is not judged by how graceful or patient I am as a person. It is not judged by how affectionate or enduring I am. Instead, it'll be based on what I look like, how I dress, how much pain I can take … and still excel at whatever it is I do. I'd like the reader to know that the reason I haven't stated my name or any dates is that my parents feel it will not reflect well on our family. It is not that they are conservative. They are right. Here in India, the same man who rapes a woman will call that woman promiscuous. So the woman loses on all fronts. She is a victim, and yet not allowed to say that she is one. I, for instance, get an opportunity to write this article, yet I can't write everything I want to or even tell you who I am. Ironic isn't it.

If one is given an identity the minute one is born, one must be given full opportunity to live that identity. I never learned what it is to be a girl, and I will probably never be a woman ... in the true sense of either word.

the reading

nikhat

When I started out to write this piece I thought the scattered bits that form me would all fit together. God knows I have enough things to say and have met enough extraordinary people to fill a book. Unfortunately though, both chronology and clarity fail me as I realize I don't know who I am. Where I come from and where I'd like to go have a fuzzy picture to them but who I am today—not too many clues.

So I decided to try out my life as a metaphor. The one that came to mind was that of a tarot card reading. We get to pick three cards from a deck, one representing our past, one our present and one the future. Just like with the cards, life's choices depend on our own will, karma, luck and of course the hands of another. I too am dividing to life into three and sharing my fate with you. My past, a girl I used to be, writings from the yesteryears. My present as I fumble in the darkness. My future and the things I cannot know but only hope to find.

As I try and find me, wait a while or pass me by.

The Card for the Past: *it's my party and I'll cry if I want to*

I dream of a white picket fence, golden retrievers and 'Honey, I'm home' for the rest of my life. Sounds familiar? Never mind, hop on for the ride in any case.

I grew up in a boarding school on an isolated hill where the main pursuit of us kids was food. What I mean by that is how to get some. Yup, as an aim that's not very traumatizing. Well, it could be, but that's another story ...

Chronology being important to me, I write about things in the order they occurred. Somehow right now it doesn't seem to matter. So losing chronology, I am giving each person or event its own space, its own passage. This way their meaning in my life will not be lost. What fun! The difference between living life and writing about it.

My parents divorced each other when I was five. I don't remember much of that time. When you're that age words like 'blocking' and 'defense mechanisms' don't mean anything to you. I got to live with my mom. What I do remember is the feeling of being abandoned. I was worried that dad left because I wasn't good enough, (clichés begin somewhere!). The point is that I missed my dad and I wanted him back.

He never came back. In all fairness to him, he was definitely around. I mean he came to see me often and there were picnics and visits to the zoo and holidays in the jungle. Somehow it wasn't quite enough. Going for sleepovers to my friends' houses became a nightmare. Their fathers came home at night to sit with their families over dinner. I, the one with verbal diarrhea simply didn't have anything to say. It would hurt too much.

My father remarried when I was eight. I refused to acknowledge that event; I wanted nothing to do with the new wife. This resolve lasted a few years but slowly I made a turnaround and grew to care for her quite a lot actually. The real bomb was dropped on me when I was twelve, and they adopted a little girl. After being an only child for so many years, I suddenly had to deal with a sister, a sister twelve years younger, one that I didn't want.

I took one look at the tiny sleeping baby and I knew I could never hate her, never resent her. It was my duty to protect her from all harm. She would never hurt like I had done. I couldn't protect her, I see her, I watch her every move when I am with her, is she going to be me?

I think I'm beginning to deal with the angst/hate/love I feel for my dad. He's the only dad he knows how to be. Do I keep that or lose that? To hold on we must let go?

My mother. My mother is like a witch's bubbling cauldron. There's a dash of newt's eye and lizard's blood but a generous sprinkling of rosemary, violets and laughter. She has always been there, right from day one, making sure that I know I count and that at least she thinks I'm pretty special. Make no mistake, very often we hate each other's guts. She is the 'pinnacle of form' and me, 'the slovenly pig'!

Sometimes I think I owe her, I owe her for not letting go. She built a life for us and that's pretty hard work. Surely I should give something back. Is this some kind of guilt, I don't know? Truth be told, there are so many layers to our relationship that I haven't the vocabulary to explain it. What I do know is that all that she wants is for me to be happy, to have a full life, a husband, career, kids, the whole deal. Hard one, mom.

I met him in my first year of college. He was the broody one who at all the parties sat in a corner nursing his drink and surveying the world with a cynical eye. Of course I was intrigued (hooked) at once! After playing cat and mouse for a month we were officially 'together', actually it was one kiss and that was that.

I was eighteen, I lost my virginity a month after we met. I have never regretted it for a moment, not then, not now. My mother warned me about that, she said that the act itself changes the relationship. Perhaps she was right, I know I loved him with an intensity that was almost unreal to me.

Sex. The word always forms so easily in my mouth. I mean, it's so much shorter and to the point than saying 'making love'. When a woman says the word (sex) she's slightly, ever so slightly, perceived as vulgar, and a man who speaks of 'making love,' a bit of a pansy. Hmmm.

Anyway, back to him. To cut a long story short, after one and a half years it was over. It just didn't work. I was devastated. There were so many questions in my mind. Did I try hard enough? Would anybody ever love me the way he had? Was it really over? So I did what I had to do, I ran. I left town for two months. A change of scene did do me some good. It gave me space to sink deeper into denial. The more I didn't think of him, the more I wanted to be with him again.

And then, I was. After seven months we were back together again. This time we were going to do it right. No games, no petty jealousy, just maturity and respect. I was so happy, he felt like home to me. Being with him was all that mattered.

It almost worked. Somewhere along those months, somehow, without us knowing, all the old issues emerged from the shadows and crept back into our lives. Then, again like the first time, one day it was over. Though, unlike then, the finality of it hit the very core of me. We had tried, tried to the utmost limit of our capabilities. He gave me all he could of himself, I know that. And I did the same, I know that too. Sometimes it was too little, sometimes too much.

In any case, I didn't run but dove right into the pain. I still haven't touched the surface and the only thing that helps me is the unshakable knowledge that this is the way it was meant to be and one day I will be able to grasp that.

You see the thing is that we couldn't be the person the other wanted us to be. Compromise is one thing, even sacrifice, but we all have one thin but unbreakable cord running through us. A cord uniquely ours, that makes us who we are. We can't change that, not for anyone.

Love is such a strange thing, just when you think you've understood it, it leaps out of your grasp. Sometimes I'm afraid of it, other times I look for it. There is only one question that often bites the back of my mind—which is harder, to find love or to make it stay?

My first encounter with death was when I was fourteen years old. My grandmother died of breast cancer. She was my 'safe place,' my *nani*. I used to feel that nothing in the world could harm me when

I was with her. There was another side to her, a side that was often engulfed in depression and anger. I never saw it, perhaps the only one who didn't. Remembering all the 'picnics' on the balcony, designer dresses for my dolls and 3:00 a.m. halwa parties, I ache for her to once again stroke my brow, chasing the frown lines away. She had the softest hands you could ever imagine, always cool and smelling faintly of Oil of Olay. A couple of months after she died I was sitting out in the sun reading. Suddenly there was a loud buzzing in my ear and I looked up to see a beautiful bumblebee sitting on my shoulder waving to me with iridescent wings. It was her. This may sound crazy but I knew, I just did. It was as if she was saying she'd always be there watching and looking out for me. To this date, whenever I see a bumblebee, it is a comforting sign, it's buzzing a song sent just for me.

When I was seventeen, I again lost someone I loved very deeply. My uncle committed suicide. I was at boarding school at the time, preparing for our Founder's Day. They didn't tell me, not until I went home for the holidays a week later. They didn't need to tell me. One look at my mother's eyes said it all.

Let me tell you a bit about him. I used to call him the family encyclopedia. All one had to do was say '1923,' and he would rattle off all that had happened in the world in that year. A genius he was often called. 'Too much heart and too much mind' a friend of the family explained to me at the funeral. 'A person like that is not of this world and can never belong here'. So he was gone and we were still here.

I guess that is what death is all about. It's always easier for the dead guy. The ones left behind are the ones affected. I know the day he took his life he took a part of ours with him.

I am not scared of death, only scared of the fact that I'm not scared. Someone said, 'Death is not the greatest loss in life. The greatest loss is what dies inside while we're still alive'. That's the truth, why fight it?

I had got into St. Stephen's college. Wow! Philosophy. Double wow!

I failed my first year exams, just like that. This time my black sense of humour didn't come to my rescue. I knew I was drowning. I had never felt so ashamed, and the humiliation of failing was more than I thought I could bear. My boyfriend tried to save me, telling me that it was going to be all right, that I was smart and that it was just bad luck. But I was in no mood to be saved. It was my mother who suggested therapy. Visions of straitjackets flashed before my eyes but at the time I was ready to grab hold of *anything*. So I went, and it helped. Hey, I'm not saying all my problems were solved. But the revelatory thing that happened was that I knew had them (my problems, I mean) and I was truly okay with that. The thing to remember is that going to therapy is like going to a bar, not only alcoholics walk in.

Anyway, I don't have all the answers; I don't want all the answers. We go about our lives chasing the bigger things, fame, money, spirituality, whatever. Hey, what about cheap thrills? Moments of pure unadulterated fun? Aren't those the ones worth living for? You figure it out. And as for me, white picket fences? Screw that, I'm off to learn the secrets of the unicorns and do a little dancing in the moonlight.

The Card for the Present: *randomness and divinity from up shit's creek*

I had a twenty-fourth birthday a few weeks ago. This was to be a milestone age, I had decided at sixteen (it sounded a lot older then). This would be when my shit would start getting together. Twenty-four with no money, no job, no boyfriend and a handful of jumbled thoughts had not been part of the plan.

I lived in London for a year and a half to do my masters degree. I moved back a few months ago. Being out there in the world meant knowing aloneness and freedom and happiness for the first time. That person is lost, I think she stayed behind. I feel sometimes—maybe more often than not—that the body should have cancelled the return ticket as well. There was a feeling I knew well there, I think it's called joyous anticipation. Every day held the promise of adventure, every stranger was a potential friend. Now things are different. I guess home is where one already knows everybody. Although it is here I am lost. Thus my present is fragmented and all I have to share with you are my thoughts and a few more secrets.

Rejection feels like a stab wound would. Swift, sharp and mockingly cruel. It has taken my breath away. When we reject, cut someone loose from our lives, there is pain, that awful feeling of guilt, but there is that lemon twizzler of relief too. I thought the one who is turned away had righteousness and rage to lend them some dignity. Am sorry, I was wrong. There is no dignity for the rejected, alas there is no rage. No one really shouts aloud in furious anger, 'How dare you not pick me!' No, it is an anguished wail (albeit a silent one) of 'Why? Why didn't you pick me?' The rejected are bewildered. What went wrong? That's when the ultimate in refined self-doubt kicks in.

I sit here wondering what it was that belonged to me that wasn't good for you. Look at me, I am a woman. I want you—I don't need you, I don't love you, I just desire you. To explore the contours of your mind, the tectonic plates of your body, the silken folds of your soul. Don't you want to know what the hollow at the elbow of my arm tastes like? What lurks behind the easy laughter, what quickens my pulse? I guess not. Is it the way I smell?

Now that I think of it, is it really you I want? Had I made an image of the person I wanted you to be and now find myself stuck in my own quicksand? I see him in you. The Byronic uncle clouded in ambiguous thought and smoke. I wanted to know him and then he was gone. Are you only a fleeting reminiscence of a memory?

Maybe you are just a porthole to the place I want to see. Although you make me laugh.

You know what really frightens me? It's the fact that I'm usually you. The one who runs away. To whom the idea of intimacy and of giving of oneself seems to be an act of weakness. You ran before I could, that is what I cannot fathom. You robbed me of my act. Before my own seeds of claustrophobia could germinate, yours took root and grew branches.

This is the cosmic revenge that I have been dreading. The karma that gets you in this lifetime. I was fickle and threw away the affections of others without a backward glance. I realize how easy it is to dismiss another, to deny a feeling. I wish I could acknowledge all those I swept away in callow smugness, respect them and thank them. You showed me that—giving of oneself happens. A part of one's soul drifts away like a renegade island and hits the shores of another's. I don't need you to acknowledge that. I think I just did.

Here I am sitting at yet another café (luckily one I've been to before) alone. I am tired of doing this by myself—worrying about everything. Really, for the first time in my life, I wish someone else would do the worrying for me. I am upset at myself, a little disappointed. This is what I did, wandering around, talking to strangers, writing. Now my batteries are running low. To be led seems an infinite luxury. Does one really need that second, that other in order to feel complete and safe? God, I was so sure of that answer once. I want to be sure again but the tiredness leads me elsewhere.

They are all getting married, my friends I mean. I blinked for a second and found myself in Alice's matrimony land. Okay, so maybe not marriage but their so-called biological clocks are beginning to hum nursery rhymes. The thing is—I don't want a child. The thought of motherhood sends a trickle of ice water down my spine. It's not that I don't like children, they're great. For heaven's sake, I studied child psychology. My dream is my own orphanage by the sea. It's the curiosity of a child that undoes me. The innocence that comes along with the sense they have that the world owes them an explanation, an intelligent well thought-out one at that.

Children aren't jaded or cynical. Some see so much hate, violence and neglect, and yet there is always the potential to love and be loved in return. It is only at adolescence, when the vocabulary kicks in, that we have the propensity to be dull and therefore incurable.

I digress, well now that it's established that kids are not the problem, it's just the thought of producing one of my own that petrifies me. Not to mention the idea of the involvement of a third party. Yes, I admit it, I have Brady Bunch phobia. What is wrong with me?

Okay, I just lied to you in a big way. It is the biggest lie I repeat to myself over and over again. I am not scared of committing myself to a child. No, it is the fear of overcommitting that paralyses me. I do not want to allow myself to love another so completely. The only unconditional love that exists in the world belongs to a mother towards her child. I know this because I see proof of it at home everyday. I will not love another being so much that their choices and failures destroy me. A lifetime of no control over the situation, for as Gibran says 'They come through you but not from you, they are with you, yet they belong not to you.' I am afraid to love only because I will love too much. I see the pain in my mother's eyes when I am weak and immobile, when I am callous and unthinking, when I allow my heart to be broken and most of all when I spit on myself. I am sorry yet I cannot help myself. I can't be the woman she wants me to be, the woman I almost am.

Talking to the women around my age and older, I find that most of them are aware of some kind of 'sell by' date before which things should be settled. They are moving towards it or at least thinking about getting there. Why can't I be like that? I don't yearn for someone to talk to for the rest of my life. No, I want someone to talk to right now. Just someone to make me laugh, not someone who might complement my eggs.

To be young and free. Aren't these the best years of my life? The mind, the body supple, they cannot belong to you, nor to you, nor to you. I am still searching. Sometimes I am so tired of waking up to it alone, again. But something inside tells me to hold on—the world has only just begun to reveal its splendors.

They say get a job, make some money, and grow some roots. I cannot, I don't know what will sustain me, keep my interest ...

But I am sure of one thing, this must be only the beginning. I search for an identity and a path to call my own. For right now I am just another girl, travelling, sometimes incognito, waiting to see it, smell it, taste it, hear it and sleep with it. All.

The Card for the Future: *and the fat lady goes on …*

The floatation theory: It is well known that a body that is dead will float in water. This leads us to conclude the following:

The worst that can happen to one while living is to be dead while living. 'Dying' is here not to be taken in its literal sense but metaphorically (always more poetic). Thereby implying the dulling of the mind and the soul and having all the fun sucked out of one. This would be real death. Therefore if one ever reached that point one must immediately begin to float back up.

Thus reaffirming one's will to live and asserting—what goes down must come up.

I made this theory up for a friend at a time when the last gap of light was running low. It works for me every time. Yes, it's silly and perhaps makes only a little sense, but then isn't it in the absurd that the truth lies? I will float back up. I know that, because every once in a while I make a good decision, for me.

tilly

tilly

The room in my head is really running out of space. I need to let some long-known inhabitants out. Should I just pick up the red cushion, settle down in the black chair and pen down my sinister black thoughts? Oh! How dramatic, a rather unnecessary prelude. What do you mean by saying, 'Should I just ... and pen down?' You have begun to write, so just finish it darling. Stop acting! Take action instead!

This is where my story begins. I have often confused acting with taking action and vice versa. The result of this gross confusion has been a false and artificial self that hangs heavy round my neck. Life demands that one play different roles, but I feel confused as to my real identity. I start with my childhood, a mature old self; my adulthood, a schizophrenic childlike self; and end with my struggle to serenade happiness just the way I am.

My paternal home had this beautiful Burmese table of carved wood with a marble top. Of the six chairs around the table, one was very special to my cousins and myself. This chair had a 'velvet cushion and a leg rest!' To occupy this throne you had simply to be the first one to sit on it. But this was more difficult than you might imagine. The number of cousins competing for the throne was no less than eight, of varying shapes and sizes. I was six years old and saved by just one cousin from being the youngest of the competitors. I hated getting up early in the morning and was not very focused or dogged about fighting for what I liked or loved. So I always lost out to my more ambitious cousins. Besides, I had about me this false air of self-sacrifice that I truly enjoyed wearing.

My grandfather never sat on that chair, but suddenly, one Kolkata-monsoon morning, he did sit down on it, ate his usual portion of two pieces of toast cut into neat squares dipped in a cup of malai-free milk. He walked out of the house with his retinue of servants and when he came back brought with him this huge business order which was going to take him to Japan. His beloved wife, a music teacher, took in this news and the absence of hilsa fish in the market in the same breath. I was too young then to understand their love. But I was old enough to know that it was special. And much later, when I fell in love for the first time in my twenty-four years, I also realized how rare their love was.

After my Granddad went to Japan, the chair became for me a passport to foreign lands and untold adventure. My vivid dreams provided the inspiration I lacked in terms of ambition and the very next day I woke up two hours earlier than my usual time. I felt like a nocturnal bird that has woken in the late evening. Adjusting myself to this new experience, I gingerly climbed into the sacred throne, which seemed not unlike Aladdin's magic carpet.

I then saw my first sunrise and it was beautiful.

You may ask how I remember a sunrise seen at six years old, but you just have to believe that I possess not the privilege of forgetting, the good or the bad. My skin was charmed by that touch of velvet. I kept stroking it with almost hypnotized movements, losing myself in its creamy softness. Much later I recognized my fetish for anything soft—silk stockings, soft hands and ears. My mind raced with thoughts of becoming a freedom fighter, not because I wanted to free anything or anyone, but because my maternal grandmother used to praise the freedom fighters, whom she had fed when they came to the house for shelter. She called them heroes. I could not understand what freedom meant nor could I spell it, but I just wanted to be a hero. In my trance I shifted gears from being a freedom fighter to being a Naxalite, not because I understood anything of their left-wing, volcanic ideology, but because I thought they lived romantic lives in forests and that people outside lived in fear of them.

People! I should have known then that my biggest enemy was going to be this desire to know what people thought of me and if they approved of the role I was playing. When I look back on that six-year-old, I feel sadness for not having experienced what people call 'innocence.' I had just started acting too soon. Why? I ask myself. Perhaps because of my chameleon-like ability to adapt to new environments, stimulated by the possibilities of a diplomatic existence. Even as a six-year-old I had mastered the art of gaining approval from diverse and even polarized groups of people. The insecurity in the depths of my soul craved approval constantly. It's not like the insecurity has now sublimated itself, but it certainly did find a positive outlet in a 'magical profession.'

For now, let's get back to the chair. My reverie was broken by the shrieking of the telephone. I was scared of getting up from my seat lest some cousin wake up and take my place. There was half an hour to breakfast and my rivals were waking up, but I refused to leave the chair, even though I needed to go to the bathroom. Not then, not now have I known how to enjoy what I love, so compelling is my insecurity.

So finally the competitors trooped into the dining room and I feigned such nonchalance. On seeing my stiff self posed on the chair, some shrieked, some grimaced, while others were simply shocked. I felt such a thrill. Raja-da was usually king of the breakfast table and if he deigned benevolence, his little sister, the pesky Rani, got to sit on the throne. Today Raja-da fumed silently at this sudden usurpation. He did not know what to do with his anger at being bettered by someone all of five years younger than him and that too an ugly little girl. He began to spill his food on the floor deliberately, saying, 'My hands are too big, they keep hitting the wall on this side of the table.' Or he pinched his little sister and said in a loud whisper, 'It's because of you that I woke up late today.'

Men can be so petty! I actually felt sorry for that pesky Rani and that idiotic Raja-da.

Why were people so selfish? Little Rani began to cry. I decide to put an end to this matter. In my most mature and grandmotherly voice I said, 'Please do stop fighting like little children. Raja-da please take the seat.' How old did I think I was, 'little children' indeed? I got up with a sigh of impatience, my head held high, following the line of Queen Victoria's neck which I had often seen on the gold guineas hidden in my grandma's drawer beneath the silver box of supari. I got up from that seat because I hated to see Rani cry, but deep in my heart I knew I also wanted to be praised and honoured for my 'great sacrifice'. I was aware of this duplicity even at the age of six. What a monster! And since that fateful day of 'great sacrifice' and 'conflict resolution' I was fondly called 'shona burri' (a darling old woman) by all adults.

This title was tweaked only slightly in school where I became the responsible agony aunt. My friends fell in and out of love and my telephone bill increased rapidly. How I would wish that not more than two would fall out of love at the same time—I really could not afford it! Did I ever wish then to fall in love myself? No way! But honestly there were moments when I did wish for someone to fall in love with me. That was an impossibility. Until the tenth grade I was the ugliest kid possible—buck teeth, a skirt that went beneath the knee and socks that climbed up to touch its hem, oiled hair, an embarrassing stammer and vacant eyes. How did the gentle metamorphosis from a gawky childhood to an aware adolescent begin? Perhaps my great grades in the board exams in the tenth for which I had studied like a maniac. Not because I loved studying, only because I thought that then even if I was ugly people would at least think me intelligent—I refused to remain a mental midget. Or perhaps it was just hormones.

From a flunky to a topper—the transition found me with new friends (of whom many were guys), a sharp wit, a much shorter skirt and a desire to express myself creatively in the performing arts. My newfound confidence was such a new feeling for me that I reveled in it with total self-absorption and hence 'seemed' self-reliant. Since most of my guy friends were tired of their girlfriends' dependence on them I became highly popular with them as the androgynous chick. Here was a new development in my many-faced existence. I was like the boys because of my self-reliance and fondness for rugby and pala (a very rough boys' game). I was like the girls because I had decent legs albeit a little short. I became the 'not beautiful but popular girl' in school.

Along with my newfound popularity I found subtle but potent changes in my body. A slight burgeoning in my flat chest, a more rounded hip were changes but the real change was a conscious effort to love my own body and mind. By self-love I do not refer to masturbatory escapades, but also to the feeling, 'You are good, baby! You are worth something!' The important thing to note is that I had to tell myself this very often. I was really addicted to the drug of attention. The high was as euphoric as the lows were abysmal. Back then in school I seemed on a high as I was getting all the attention I had so thirsted for. The façade of confidence was incredibly fragile. I was so lonely and thought the only way out was to get a guy to 'love' me.

Lo and behold! The universe must have heard the prayers of this messed-up kid and I landed myself a boyfriend without even seeking one. You know how it works in schools, right? A girlfriend kept giving me non-subtle hints about Akbar liking me and the same girl went and told Akbar that I liked him. And before I knew it the whole school was talking about Akbar's latest girlfriend. I was at a crossroads. Should I hold on to the independence of being the cool single chick who is everyone's friend or be the girlfriend of this tall, goodlooking basketball player, the dream of every girl in school? I chose the latter, my first mistake.

So I had a boyfriend. It was such a pain. I had to spend a lot of time with him during school and to stand with him in the cafeteria during the lunch break even if I had nothing to say to him—this was the protocol. Damn it! Even though I did not like him much I just could not get over the fact that he wanted me as his girlfriend. Our school was full of the prettiest girls one could find and, without pretending to be modest, I was certainly one of the most ugly. My double self reared its ugly head again. I was so touched by this guy's ability to have 'fallen in love' with 'me.' He had said so in a letter sent in a cream envelope along with the silver chain he used to wear round his neck. I wore the chain round my neck and bound myself to love him forever even if I did not much like him and found him intellectually impoverished.

This was twenty days after I had begun my pretence of being in love with Big Moose. Before thirty were over I was quite sure that I would marry him and we would make babies together. You might think me hasty, but Hell, I forgot to tell you an important milestone in this relationship. A kiss, or rather, something close to a kiss was exchanged at my first late-night party. The guy nibbled the edge of my lips and there was an utter mismatch of speed and mis-aiming of tongues. Though I found it physically most unexciting, it was mentally arousing, as, darlings, it was my first kiss ever!

My boyfriend came to visit me at home and figured we were not rich in the least. Now that was a big disappointment for this rich kid. But I thought love transcended all barriers—caste, creed, class, the lack of a Mercedes Benz and of holidays abroad. So while I was busy mentally sketching the design of our little cottage by the seaside, my dear boyfriend was busy writing love letters to a new rich girl in school. The poor guy did not have the guts to break my heart by telling me that it was all over, but then he did need his silver chain back. We have to be practical after all, can't survive on love and fresh air. After all these years when I look back on that one month of my life—I feel like kicking my ass. But tell me why he dumped me? Was it because I was not rich or because I was ugly or was I just impossible to love? Maybe it was none of the above or perhaps all. Who cares?

This minor infatuation was truly insignificant in terms of heartbreak. I was up on my feet and raring to go within a week. It was also the end of school and I never saw this guy again. I vowed never to get involved again, and did not for the next seven long, important years of my life. In those seven years I built a fortress around me that not even a sliver of light could enter. What or who made me fall in love and trespassed on my life after those seven years, I will talk of later or maybe

I won't. But let me tell you the discoveries of the sacred seven years. These seven years were the start of a journey that led me to discover the 'magical profession.'

I entered the College Special to Lady Shri Ram dressed in highly stylish ethnic wear (my only decent dress). I was a fresher going to face my first day of college, but I hid all my anxieties and insecurities beneath an elusive and distant facial expression. It was a charming performance indeed. Two pretty, highly nervous, Punjabi girls asked me if I was Head of the Department of Sociology! I hid my surprise and coolly replied 'Not yet!' I went and sat on the last seat hidden from rest of the bus and looked nervously out of the window. An old woman with a kind face and a badly cut salwar kameez sat down next to me. After a while she asked me which school I was in. I replied, 'I am in college.' What range! Who the hell am I? Am I the 'shona buri' of yesteryear transformed into a Sociology lecturer or the vulnerable heartbroken schoolgirl pretending to be an indifferent young woman? The penny drops, I am everything and perhaps more. It dropped as silently as a pin on the carpeted floor of my college auditorium. And the curtains rose on my first stage performance in a shadow play based on Rasasundari Debi's *Amar Jiban*.

Back in the 1840s in Kolkata, a young lady called Rasasundari Debi taught herself in secrecy to read and wrote the first female autobiography in Bangla (*Amar Jiban*). I have heard of her since childhood from my dearest Amma. Inspired by Rasasundari Debi, my grandmother taught herself music in spite of family opposition and made a living out of it! (How dare she! they said).

The stealthy cultivation of certain sensibilities in oneself is an unknown stranger to me. And yet I played the part on stage. This was the beginning of wearing masks that were legitimate. They ranged from Sarbajaya, a poor, caste-conscious Brahmin woman; Dolka Bai, a Maharashtran gypsy molested in police custody; Alice, a Bihari maidserant; Kalyani, a victim of incest; Deepa, a Bengali woman with two kids who is betrayed by her lover ... These were creative extensions of my being. However, unlike the imaginary escapades at age six on the velvet chair, I now felt the story of each part I played as a way towards understanding the world and facets of myself better. And guess what I found? There just are so many sides to my being and that's not so bad is it? The reason for my multiple identities is largely that I did what I felt like doing when I felt like doing it. The sheer freedom has not lessened the desire to learn, but has created an octopus-being with the ability to spread tentacles to various realms.

The dappled life of an actor, with its mixed shades of fame and anonymity, did more than legitimize my schizophrenic existence. I did not have to sit on any special chair to conjure up a beautiful mirage, I just carried an imaginary velvet chair with me wherever I went. Akin to the proverbial Gandhian cave, my imaginary chair is a symbol of happiness in being just the way I am. Perhaps then the 'magical profession' is not 'acting/taking action' but simply learning to love your self a little.